YOU CHOOSE BOOKS

WORLD WAR II

An Interactive History Adventure

by Elizabeth Raum

Consultant:
William O. Oldson, Founder and Director
Institute on World War II and the Human Experience
Florida State University

Capstone *press*®

Mankato, Minnesota

Library of Congress Cataloging-in-Publication Data
Raum, Elizabeth.
　　World War II : an interactive history adventure / by Elizabeth Raum.
　　p. cm. — (You choose books)
　　Includes bibliographical references and index.
　　Summary:"Describes the events of World War II and explains the significance of the war
today. The reader's choices reveal the historical details from the perspective of a member of the
Dutch resistance, a Canadian soldier, and an American soldier" — Provided by publisher.
　　ISBN-13: 978-1-4296-2344-5 (hardcover)
　　ISBN-13: 978-1-4296-3457-1 (softcover)
　　ISBN-13: 978-1-4296-4267-5 (softcover)
　　1. World War, 1939–1945 — Juvenile literature. I. Title.
D743.7.R38 2009
940.53 — dc22   2008028916

Editorial Credits

Megan Schoeneberger, editor; Juliette Peters, set designer; Gene Bentdahl, book designer;
　　Wanda Winch, photo researcher

Photo Credits

AP Images, 37, 78, 96; AP Images/Henry L. Griffin, 104; AP Images/U.S. Marine Corps,
cover; AP Images/U.S. Signal Corps, 103; Getty Images Inc./AFP, 32; Getty Images Inc./
Hulton Archive, 86; Getty Images Inc./Hulton Archive/Keystone, 15, 52; Getty Images
Inc./Hulton Archive/MPI, 85, 100; Getty Images Inc./Popperfoto, 51; Getty Images Inc./
Popperfoto/Paul Popper, 73; Getty Images Inc./Time & Life Pictures/William Vandivert, 58;
Getty Images Inc./Time Life Pictures/Dmitri Kessel, 66; Getty Images Inc./Time Life Pictures/
John Florea, 98; Getty Images Inc./Time Life Pictures/Mansell, 6; Getty Images Inc./Time
Life Pictures/Timepix/Hugo Jaeger, 10, 27; Getty Images Inc./Time Life Pictures/William
C. Shrout, 71; Library of Congress, Prints & Photographs Division, FSA/OWI Collection,
40; National Archives and Records Administration (NARA), 46, 55; National Archives
and Records Administration (NARA)/Boyle (Army), 74; National Archives and Records
Administration (NARA)/Sgt. Thomas D. Barnett Jr. (Marine Corps), 93; Naval Historical
Center/photo by Warrant Officer Obie Newcomb Jr., (USMCR), 82; United States Holocaust
Memorial Museum, Bep Meyer Zion (The views expressed in this book and the context in
which the image is used do not necessarily reflect the views or policy of, nor imply approval or
endorsement by, the USHMM), 21

The author would like to dedicate this book to her father, Staff Sergeant Charlie Fletcher, a tank driver who
served in Europe with the 191st Tank Battalion (1942–1945); her father-in-law, Sergeant Howard Raum, an
Army x-ray technician stationed at Oliver General Hospital, Augusta, Georgia (1942–1945); and his brother,
Corporal Robert Raum, a cannoneer in the 194th Field Artillery Battalion killed in France, January 14, 1945.

TABLE OF CONTENTS

ABOUT YOUR ADVENTURE

YOU are living in the late 1930s. More than 20 years have passed since World War I. Now conflicts in Europe and Japan are building up again. Will there be another world war?

In this book, you'll explore how the choices people made meant the difference between life and death. The events you'll experience happened to real people.

Chapter One sets the scene. Then you choose which path to read. Follow the directions at the bottom of each page. The choices you make will change your outcome. After you finish one path, go back and read the others for new perspectives and more adventures.

YOU CHOOSE the path
you take through history.

Many Germans saluted Adolf Hitler as the leader of their country.

War!

"Look!" your brother says, holding up the newspaper on September 1, 1939. In black letters are the words "German Army Invades Poland."

Germany was not pleased with the peace that followed World War I (1914–1918). The country lost the war, and many Germans believed they were treated unfairly.

Adolf Hitler became the leader of Germany in 1933. He and his political party, the Nazis, blame Germany's problems on the last war. They also blame the Jews, a group of people descended from ancient Hebrews. Hitler believes the Jews are a weaker race than the white German race. "A stronger race will drive out the weak," he writes.

Turn the page.

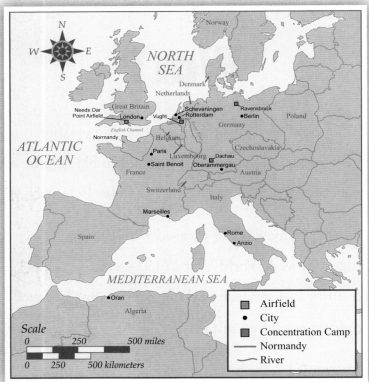

Hitler promises to make Germany powerful
again. He began in 1938 by taking over Austria.
In March 1939, Hitler seized Czechoslovakia.
And now his army has invaded Poland.

"There's fighting in Asia too," your brother says. "The Japanese are attacking China."

The leader of Italy, Benito Mussolini, vows to help Germany gain power in Europe. In 1940, Japan joins Germany and Italy to form the Axis powers.

Poland, Great Britain, France, India, Australia, and New Zealand hope to stop the Axis. Together they are known as the Allied forces, or Allies.

"Will there be another world war?" you ask.

"I'm afraid so," your father says. Sooner or later, you'll have to decide what role to play.

➛ To join the forces fighting the Germans in the Netherlands, turn to page **11**.

➛ To sign up for the Canadian military, turn to page **41**.

➛ To serve with the American armed forces, turn to page **67**.

German bombs destroyed the city of Rotterdam, the Netherlands, in May 1940.

CHAPTER 2

War in the Netherlands

Early Friday morning, May 10, 1940, you awake to the sound of popping noises filling the air. "What's going on?" you ask.

"Those are German planes!" your brother shouts, pointing to the sky. "They're shooting at our planes."

"But the Netherlands is neutral. We aren't part of the war."

"That doesn't matter to Hitler," your brother says. "First he attacked Poland, then Norway and Denmark. Now he's coming after us."

Turn the page.

The Germans are heavily armed with tanks and bombers. The small Dutch Army has no tanks. Their planes are old. They ride bicycles and carry outdated guns. Outnumbered and outmatched, the Dutch Army does its best to hold off the Germans. After three days, the Germans control most of the country. But the major cities are still under Dutch control.

On May 14, Germans drop bomb after bomb on the city of Rotterdam. The city is destroyed. More than 900 people, including your cousin, are killed in the attack. The next day, the Dutch government surrenders to the Germans.

That night, your family gathers around the radio. London's radio station, the BBC, reports that Queen Wilhelmina and the Dutch government have left the Netherlands for England. "Why has she left us in our time of need?" you ask.

"She must have good reasons, my daughter. Someday we'll understand," Father says.

When German soldiers march through the streets, you stand on the sidewalk and sob. Your cousin is dead, and your country is no longer free.

Some of your neighbors support the Germans by joining the Dutch Nazi Party. Others welcome German soldiers into their homes. Not you and your family. You want nothing to do with the Nazis.

Soon the Nazis' secret police, the Gestapo, begin making rules. First they make it illegal to listen to the BBC. Then they order citizens to turn in their radios.

"We'll keep our radio," your father says.

13

Turn the page.

It's dangerous. If the Germans find the radio, your father could be arrested.

"They won't find it," he says. He cuts a hole in the wall. Then he moves the radio, which is the size of a small dresser, into that space. A bookshelf hides the lower half. He hangs a mirror over the top part.

Every night, you listen to broadcasts from the Dutch government in England. It is the only news you trust.

Your brother begins a secret newspaper to report what you hear on the radio. "Will you help me deliver copies to the neighbors?" he asks.

It is dangerous work. If you are caught, you will be arrested. And the Nazis kill traitors.

➤ To help deliver the newspapers, go to page 15.

➤ To refuse to help, turn to page 17.

Queen Wilhelmina of the Netherlands was forced to flee to London at the beginning of World War II.

"Of course, I'll help," you say.

"Be careful to avoid the homes of Nazi supporters," he reminds you.

You and your brother join a group of young people who resist the Nazis. You go out after dark and write OZO, the Dutch abbreviation for "Orange will conquer," on nearby walls. The Germans have forbidden any mention of the royal family or their royal color, orange.

Turn the page.

One day, a German soldier stops you as you are walking home. "What is this jewelry you are wearing?" he says. He points to a 10-cent silver coin pinned to your shirt. The coin has a picture of Queen Wilhelmina on the front. "It is against the law to display the queen's picture," he says. He tears the coin away. "Go quickly before I arrest you. I'll be watching you."

You tell your brother what happened. "That's enough," he says. "I'm going to England. I'll help the queen and the Dutch government take the Netherlands back from the Germans. Come with me."

You've heard others talk of going to England. You're tempted to go, but your parents are getting old. If you leave, they'll be alone.

➤ To go to England, turn to page **18**.

➤ To stay with your parents, turn to page **20**.

"It's too dangerous," you say.

"If you feel that way, it's better you don't help," your brother answers. "Fear won't help the resistance."

You take classes at the university. You try to ignore German soldiers in the streets. If you just mind your own business, everything will be all right. Whenever you hear planes overhead, you pray that it is Allied soldiers coming to save the Netherlands.

In April 1943, the Germans force all university students to sign a loyalty oath. Those who don't sign must leave school.

↠ *To refuse to sign, turn to page* **19**.

↠ *To sign, turn to page* **39**.

"Go to England," your father says. "We are old. We'll be fine here, but you young people will be safer in England."

You go with your brother to a farming area near the coast. On a moonless night, a man you trust guides you to a rickety old boat. Seven of you will use it to cross the English Channel.

"There are German lookout posts along the entire Dutch coast. Go directly out to sea. And be careful," your guide says.

"I'm worried," you say. "I'm not a good swimmer. If the boat sinks, I'll drown."

The guide invites you to stay on the coast. "We do what we can to help from here."

"It's up to you," your brother says. "I'm going."

➤ *To stay in the Netherlands, turn to page* **23**.

➤ *To go to England, turn to page* **36**.

One of your professors declares, "We must resist this demand to sign an oath." He's your favorite professor and a man of courage. You refuse to sign.

A classmate takes you aside. "I feel I can trust you," she says. "We need young women to help in the resistance. Most of our young men have been shipped to work camps in the Soviet Union. It's dangerous work, but we try to get information to England. We also rescue Allied pilots. Come to the coast with me."

❧ *To help in the resistance, turn to page* **23.**
❧ *To stay in the city with your parents, turn to* **38.**

"I'll stay. I won't leave my homeland," you say.

Soon the Germans make laws that discriminate against Jewish people. Jews cannot go to the park. They cannot play sports. They can't even walk on the sunny side of the street. Jews are beaten, and their property is destroyed.

By late 1941, many Jews know that they must leave the country or go into hiding. If they don't, they risk being killed by the Nazis. Leaving the Netherlands is impossible. Germany controls all of the surrounding land.

Some Jews hide in apartments or homes in the cities. Farms make even better hiding places. Many Dutch farmers are willing to place their own families in danger to hide Jews.

You join Group HEIN, named after the Dutch initials for the phrase, "helping others in need." The group helps Jews hide from the Nazis.

More than 20 Jews crowded into this tiny bunker to hide from the Germans.

Your job is to bike from farm to farm. You pick up letters at one farm and deliver them to the next. The Germans have taken most bikes. They use the parts for weapons, especially the rubber tires. You ride an ancient bike with rolled garden hoses for tires.

Like others in the group, you use a false name and a fake ID. That way, if you are found, the Nazis will not hurt your family.

Turn the page.

One day, as you bike from one farm to another, you spot a German checkpoint ahead. You think about turning back. But your fake ID is new. The Jewish printer who made it does good work. Do you dare go through the roadblock? If you turn back, you'll have to go miles out of your way.

➤ To go through the checkpoint, turn to page **31**.

➤ To turn back, turn to page **34**.

Your country needs your help in the resistance. The group's headquarters are at a farm near the North Sea. A powerful radio sends messages back and forth from England. One night, the group gathers around the radio operator. He receives a secret message.

"Allied planes will fly over tomorrow night," he says. "They'll drop weapons and bundles of an illegal newspaper called *The Flying Dutchman*."

You go with the group to a nearby field. Two men signal the planes with flashlights.

Something lands by your feet. You grab the bundle of newspapers. Four strong men carry a trunk filled with guns. "Come quickly!" one of them says. "We'll go to a safe house in town."

Turn the page.

But a German soldier stands guard on the bridge into town. One of the men tells you to go talk to the soldier. "While he's busy trying to impress you, we'll sneak past him."

"No," another says. "That's too dangerous. We'll hide in the shed back in the field and try again another night."

❖ To return to the field to hide, go to page 25.

❖ To volunteer to distract the guard, turn to page 27.

It's safer to hide. German soldiers must have seen the Allied planes. They are searching for you. It is a miracle they don't find you. By 4:00 in the morning, the German patrols are gone. You haul the guns and newspapers back to the farm.

You hide everything in a farm wagon beneath a load of stinky cow manure. German soldiers won't bother to dig through the manure looking for hidden weapons. The farmer delivers the papers to your a safe house in town.

By 1943, food is scarce in the Netherlands. Everyone uses ration cards to buy groceries. It's a fair way to distribute food. But people who are hiding cannot get ration cards. They depend on fake ration cards and false ID cards. As a Dutch girl, you have freedom to travel. Your job is to carry fake papers to people in hiding.

Turn the page.

Today you must take forged papers to a farm where 20 people are hiding. Some are Jewish. Some are Dutch men who have refused to join the German Army or work in German factories. Without ration cards, these people will starve.

As you bike along, you see a German roadblock up ahead. Since the Germans arrived, everyone must carry official identification papers. Your papers are fake. You use a false name. If you are arrested using your real name, your parents might be put in jail too.

You've never used your fake papers before. If there is an error, you could be arrested. Do you trust your papers enough to go through the roadblock, or should you turn back?

→ To go through the checkpoint, turn to page **31**.

→ To turn back, turn to page **34**.

German troops guarded streets during the German occupation of the Netherlands.

"I'll distract the guard," you whisper. One of the men takes your newspapers. You walk along the bridge. "Halt!" the guard says in German. He asks for your identification.

Slowly, you reach into your pocket. The first pocket is empty.

Turn the page.

"Now!" the soldier roars. You smile sweetly at him and shrug as if you don't mean to cause harm. Finally you hand over your papers. You have managed to turn the guard so that his back is to the bridge. You see your friends sneak safely past. He hands you back your papers. "Where are you going?" he asks.

"To my aunt's house. Soldiers took my bicycle, so I had to walk. It took me longer than I expected."

"I will walk you to your aunt's house," the soldier says. But you have no aunt in this town.

➤ To let the soldier walk you to town, go to page **29**.

➤ To run away, turn to page **33**.

You wait for the soldier to walk with you. What can you do?

"Which house?" the German asks. You point to a narrow house nestled between two bigger, taller houses. "There," you say, praying that whoever is there will take you in.

The German marches to the door and knocks. An elderly woman answers. She looks from you to the soldier.

"Auntie!" you say, trying to keep your voice from shaking. Can she understand that you need her protection?

She does! She reaches out and hugs you. The soldier turns to leave. Once he is gone, your "aunt" shuts the door. You thank her for her kindness.

"It's nothing," she says. "Go in peace." You slip out a back door and join the others at a safe house.

Turn the page.

It becomes more and more difficult to get food. Everyone must use ration cards at stores to purchase food. But people who are hiding, whether they are Jewish or Dutch, do not have cards. Luckily, a Jewish man who is hiding at a nearby farm makes cards that look real. Your job is to pick up the ration cards from him.

One day, you are biking back to the secret headquarters. You have an envelope full of false ration cards. But up ahead, you spot a German checkpoint. If they catch you with the cards, they'll put you in prison. You could toss the cards in a nearby ditch and go through the checkpoint. Or you could turn around. Then you would be able to deliver the ration cards. But you'd have to bike miles out of the way.

➤ *To go through the checkpoint, go to page* **31**.

➤ *To turn around, turn to page* **34**.

Your ID card is new, and the forger does good work, so you go ahead toward the checkpoint. But when the Gestapo officer checks your ID, he laughs and calls another officer over.

"Come with me," he says. He can tell your ID is fake. "You are under arrest."

You are sent by train to a prison in Scheveningen. This city is on the coast of the North Sea. There are two sections of the camp. One is for Jews, and one is for political prisoners like you.

Every Tuesday and Thursday, more Jews arrive. The Germans are rounding them up from all over the Netherlands. From here, the Germans send them to Poland. You hear the Jewish children crying. How terrible it must be for entire families to be jailed just because they are Jewish.

Turn the page.

Female prisoners were forced to work at Ravensbruck concentration camp.

In June 1944, you are moved to the Vught concentration camp. In Vught, you make rope for the German Army. Without enough food, many women become sick. On September 6, 1944, you are sent to the Ravensbruck concentration camp in Germany. This camp is even worse than Vught. You die there of starvation on May 4, 1945. It is only four days before the war in Europe ends.

THE END

To follow another path, turn to page 9.
To read the conclusion, turn to page 101.

The second the soldier looks away, you run. You hear a bullet whiz by your ear. It will be better if the soldier shoots you than takes you alive. If you are dead, you cannot tell secrets that will lead the Germans to find others in the resistance. You keep running. Another bullet whizzes past. Then another. The fourth hits its mark. You fall to the ground and bleed to death in the street. Your only comfort is that no one will discover your secrets.

THE END

To follow another path, turn to page 9.
To read the conclusion, turn to page 101.

It's safer to bike back the way you came. You are tired by the time you reach the farm where you live.

The next day, gunfire and bombing wake you up. You join others who are hiding in the basement. "We don't know what's happening," a young mother says, clutching her baby in her arms.

"All we can do is wait," you tell her. "And pray."

After three days of constant noise, there is silence. What is happening? Someone has to go see.

→ To remain inside, go to page **35**.

→ To volunteer to go outside, turn to page **37**.

The farmer says he will go. His wife begs him to wait. They have four young children. He brushes aside her concern and leaves. Then you hear gunshots.

You rush to the door. The farmer stands next to the house, safe. A German soldier lies dead in the yard. An Allied soldier stands over him, holding a rifle. You rush forward and hug the soldier. "Thank you. Thank you. You have come at last!" you say.

Other soldiers march past the farm. At long last, the Netherlands is free. The soldiers have more fighting ahead of them, but for you, the war is finally over.

THE END

To follow another path, turn to page 9.
To read the conclusion, turn to page 101.

"We'll be fine," your brother says. "It's what Father wants."

You climb into the crowded little boat. Then a German submarine, called a U-boat, appears in the distance. What if they see you? But the U-boat disappears beneath the surface.

Just when you feel safe, you notice that your feet are wet. The boat is leaking. You try to bail out water with a small tin cup. But the water keeps pouring into the boat. Some of the others dive into the sea to try to swim home. But it's too far for you. "You go," you say to your brother, but he refuses. You die together in the cold water off the coast of your beloved Netherlands.

THE END

To follow another path, turn to page 9.
To read the conclusion, turn to page 101.

Citizens in Utrecht, the Netherlands, welcomed Allied troops to their city in May 1945.

You rush outside. Tanks roll by. Canadian soldiers march behind them. They are searching for any remaining German troops. "We'll clear them out," a soldier tells you. You run and tell the others. Everyone pours out of the house. It is the first time in months that they have been able to wander outside. They cry for joy. So do you!

THE END

To follow another path, turn to page 9.
To read the conclusion, turn to page 101.

You stay in the city to help your parents. Every day, you worry that the Gestapo will come after you and your parents. You've done nothing wrong. But your brother's actions with the resistance group have put you in danger.

By the winter of 1944, food is scarce. You, your mother, and your father have ration cards. But even with the cards, there's not enough food to go around. You even dig up Father's favorite tulip bulbs and cook them. They taste like potatoes.

Finally in April 1945, Allied troops march into your city. The Germans have lost. On New Year's Day, 1946, you get bad news. Your brother died in Germany's Dachau concentration camp in January 1945. You'll never forget him or his bravery.

THE END

To follow another path, turn to page 9.
To read the conclusion, turn to page 101.

Some people speak against signing the pledge. But your parents keep saying that the war will soon be over. "We've already lost your brother to the resistance," they say. "We need to know that one of our children is safe." You sign.

Food grows scarce at the end of the war. But thanks to your ration cards, you survive. At last, in April 1945, Allied tanks roll into town. The Germans surrender. You are free.

But your joy disappears when you learn that your brother was captured. He was tried as a traitor and shipped to a concentration camp in Germany. He died there. Everyone calls him a hero. You wish you could have been as brave as he was.

THE END

To follow another path, turn to page 9.
To read the conclusion, turn to page 101.

Prime Minister Mackenzie King led Canada through World War II.

CHAPTER 3

Canada Fights for Victory

On September 3, 1939, Great Britain, France, Australia, and New Zealand declare war on Germany. On September 10, the Canadian Parliament also declares war on Germany. You listen to Prime Minister Mackenzie King's speech on the radio. "I appeal to my fellow Canadians to unite in a national effort to save from destruction all that makes life itself worth living," he says.

King's speech inspires you. Canada needs volunteers to serve in the armed forces.

41

➤ To join the Winnipeg Grenadiers, *an army division, turn to page* **42**.

➤ To join the Royal Canadian Air Force, *turn to page* **45**.

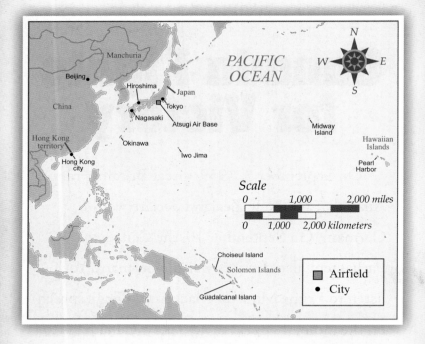

On September 30, 1939, you sign on with the Winnipeg Grenadiers. In May, you go to Jamaica to guard German prisoners of war (POWs) being held there.

In October 1941, your unit joins men from the Royal Rifles, a Signal Corps unit from Quebec. You are assigned to the cargo ship *Awatea*. There are 1,975 soldiers aboard from all over Canada.

"We're going to the British territory of Hong Kong," an officer announces. "Japanese forces are threatening to invade Hong Kong island."

On November 16, 1941, the ship docks in the city of Hong Kong. You begin training to learn how to survive on the mountainous island.

Early on December 8, sirens wail. Japanese planes bomb the harbor. You fire back. "Why are they bombing?" you ask.

"Yesterday the Japanese attacked Pearl Harbor in Hawaii. Canada, the United States, and Great Britain declared war on the Japanese," an officer says. "We're the first Canadians to join the fight."

The Japanese try to take over Mount Butler on Hong Kong Island. On December 19, Sergeant Major J. R. Osborn leads you into the dark fog to defend the island.

Turn the page.

For three hours, you fight the Japanese troops. But they outnumber you, and they have better weapons. You take cover in a ditch. "Stay down," an officer yells. "You'll be safe if you don't leave this trench. Help is on the way."

Japanese soldiers toss grenades at you. Sergeant Major Osborn catches several and throws them back, saving the lives of his men. Then a grenade falls where he can't get it.

"Grenade!" he shouts as he falls on top of it. The grenade explodes, killing Osborn. Just then, you hear a friend yell, "Help me! I've been shot."

To follow orders and stay in the trench, turn to page **46**.

To go to your friend's aid, turn to page **63**.

You decide to become a pilot and join the Royal Canadian Air Force (RCAF). You report to Elementary Flying Training School at Chatham, New Brunswick. The RCAF needs pilots as badly as it needs planes. You learn to fly whatever old planes are available. You earn your wings at the No. 9 Service Flying Training School at Summerside, Prince Edward Island. Then it's off to Scotland for more training.

British pilots introduce you to a new plane, the Hawker Typhoon. It's a low-wing, single-seater fighter plane with extra armor.

"We call them Tiffies," a British pilot tells you. "We're still testing them. Want to take a test flight?" You hesitate. There are rumors that the Tiffies have problems.

➤ To take the test flight, turn to page 48.

➤ To refuse, turn to page 50.

Allied soldiers surrendered to Japanese forces in the Pacific.

You follow orders and wait in the protected trench. An Australian soldier pulls your wounded friend to safety. The Japanese call for you to surrender. You have no choice. Before you surrender, you take apart your rifle and throw the parts into the jungle.

On December 25, after more than 17 days of fighting, all of Hong Kong falls to the Japanese. You are now a prisoner of war.

After several days, the Japanese move you to your abandoned barracks. The Japanese have taken over your camp and turned it into a prison. The buildings are a mess. Everything has been looted. The townspeople took everything they could use.

Food is scarce. Supper is just three very hard biscuits, called hardtack. You also have a few spoonfuls of canned beef called bully.

In basic training, you were told to escape if you were captured. One day, the Japanese commander brings you a paper. It says that you will promise not to try to escape. He wants you to sign it. Everyone seems to be signing. It's the smart thing to do. But isn't it your duty to escape?

➤ To sign the promise, turn to page **64**.

➤ To refuse to sign, turn to page **65**.

"I'll test the plane," you say. You soar over the countryside. Then you begin to yawn. Why are you feeling so sleepy? You struggle to stay awake, but you can't. Your body goes limp, and you lose control of the plane. The plane crashes into a farm field.

The farmer who finds you is amazed you're still alive. "What happened?" he asks. But you don't know.

It takes engineers several weeks to find out what happened. A gas called carbon monoxide leaked into the cockpit from the engine. The gas acted like a sleeping pill. That's not the only problem with the Tiffies. Several other pilots die when wings fall off and engines fail during flights. To your relief, engineers finally solve the problems.

You begin flying across the English Channel to patrol the coast of Europe. German beach patrols aim guns at the sky. Unless you stay high, you'll be hit. When you get the signal from your commander, you lower the plane to 4,000 feet. Then you drop two 1,000-pound bombs. You see them explode and hope they hit enemy targets.

As you head home, an enemy aircraft follows. You zigzag to avoid his firing guns. Then you hear the screech of metal tearing. Is it a wing? An engine? One of your buddies covers you from behind. "Got him!" he yells over the radio. Your plane shakes, but it's still flying. Maybe you can make it home. But what if you can't?

➤ To parachute out, turn to page **53**.
➤ To fly back to England, turn to page **62**.

You decide to let others test the planes, and you're glad you did. You hear of wings falling off and engines failing during test flights. Several pilots are killed.

In time, engineers work out the problems with the Hawker Typhoons. You begin flying over the English Channel, bombing German supply boats.

Bombing boats is not enough to win the war. Troops must land in France and attack the Germans on the ground. In April 1944, you go to an airfield at Needs Oar Point in England. From there, you join 11,000 planes flying to France.

You are clearing the way for thousands of soldiers to land on the beaches of Normandy. This region is in northern France. Countless bombs destroy radar and communication stations. The rat-tat-tat of anti-aircraft guns fills the air.

Troops arrived on French beaches on June 6, 1944.

By 5:00 in the morning on June 6, 1944, 5,000 boats wait offshore. Troops storm the beach. The landing is called D-Day. By nightfall, 156,000 Allied troops have reached shore.

The Germans are surprised, but they fight back. German soldiers begin firing on the Allies from hills above the beach. Many British, Canadian, and American soldiers lose their lives on the beaches of Normandy.

Turn the page.

Allied forces flew Hawker Typhoons during battles over France.

On June 29, you are flying one of 10 Typhoons over France. At least 20 German Messerschmitt Bf 109s are chasing you. Rat-tat-tat! You fire back and climb higher. Enemy gunfire hits your plane. You go into a spin. You pull out of the spin and manage to keep the plane in the air. Then the engine begins to vibrate.

➻ *To parachute out, turn to page* **56**.

➻ *To try to reach the airstrip at the beach,*
turn to page **57**.

52

You parachute out over enemy territory and land in a farm field. You check your escape kit. It contains a water bottle, chocolate, and pills to keep you awake. It also has a needle and thread, a fishhook, a compass, a map, and a list of French, German, and Spanish words.

Suddenly you hear voices. What language are they speaking? It's not French or German, and you're too far north for Spanish. You lay low, waiting. Finally a woman whispers in English, "Hello, pilot, we can help."

➤ To trust the woman, turn to page **54**.

➤ To stay hidden, turn to **55**.

You step out from behind the tree. "We are Dutch," the woman says. "We will help you find your way home." They take you to a farmhouse and show you the weapons they have gathered. "We fight the Germans any way we can," they tell you.

Two nights later, they take you to meet a French partisan group who guides you to Spain. From Spain, a neutral country, you fly to England. You fly many more missions before Germany surrenders on May 7, 1945. The war in Europe ends the next day. You return home to Canada as a hero.

THE END

To follow another path, turn to page 9.
To read the conclusion, turn to page 101.

Nazi soldiers were heavily armed.

You wait and listen. The voices fade away. Then you hear men speaking German. A man passes so close you can see the shine of his rifle in the moonlight. You don't dare breathe.

You wait several minutes. The voices move away, so you stand up. You find yourself looking directly into the face of a young German soldier. He seems as surprised as you are.

➤ To stay where you are, turn to page **60**.

➤ To run, turn to page **61**.

You jump out of the plane. Your white parachute is an easy target for German rifles. Bullets pierce your parachute, and you crash onto the beach. Pain shoots through your leg.

A medic rushes to your side. "Your leg is broken," he says.

You are brought to a hospital in England. As your leg heals, you are given light duty at the air base. You stay there until the war ends in 1945. You finish your military service and return home.

THE END

To follow another path, turn to page 9.
To read the conclusion, turn to page 101.

"It's not far to safety," you say. "I can do it." But the entire plane begins to shake. You're shaking too as you grip the control stick. You pray that you can keep the plane in the air until you reach the airstrip near the beach.

By some miracle, you reach the airstrip. You make a bumpy landing, but you are safe. Relieved, you stagger out of the cockpit.

When the ground crew checks the plane, they find several bullet holes in the blades of your propellers. As soon as your plane is repaired, you fly more missions over France.

Allied troops advance through northwestern Europe, reclaiming territory from the Germans. You fly ahead, bombing German tanks and artillery.

Turn the page.

As the Allies push farther inland, they reclaim an airstrip in France. It becomes your new base. From this airstrip, you fly missions into Germany, dropping bombs on German cities.

Many German cities, including Berlin, were destroyed by bombs during the war.

It's the most difficult thing you've ever done. You know your bombs may be killing German women and children. But you do it anyway. War is a terrible thing. The sooner it ends, the fewer lives that will be lost.

The Germans surrender on May 7, 1945. On May 8, the war in Europe officially ends. At long last, you return to Canada. You stay in the Air Force and train young pilots. You hope that they'll never have to fight another world war.

THE END

To follow another path, turn to page 9.
To read the conclusion, turn to page 101.

Seconds later, German soldiers surround you. They take you to a stalag in Germany. The prison camp is surrounded by barbed wire. German soldiers man the guard towers. Twice a day, they give you thin, tasteless soup and black bread. You struggle to keep warm in the freezing barracks.

You and the other prisoners try to make the best of a bad situation. When the weather is good, you play baseball in the yard.

You are finally released when the war ends in 1945. Getting home renews your health and your spirit.

60

THE END

To follow another path, turn to page 9.
To read the conclusion, turn to page 101.

You run and dodge. A bullet whizzes past you, but you keep going. The German shouts. He shoots again and misses. Maybe you have a chance. As you run, you look over your shoulder. Is he still behind you? No. But another German steps out of the woods and shoots you in the chest. You die in a farm field far from home.

THE END

To follow another path, turn to page 9.
To read the conclusion, turn to page 101.

It's only a short flight across the English Channel to your air base. At first, the Tiffie flies well, but then the shaking worsens. What's wrong? The engine sputters. You try to gain control, but the plane plunges into the sea. You die on impact.

THE END

To follow another path, turn to page 9.
To read the conclusion, turn to page 101.

You go to your friend's aid. You urge him to crawl back to the trench, but he dies in your arms. You have no choice but to leave him there. During a break in the shooting, you dash back to the trench. But you are not fast enough. An enemy bullet kills you before you reach safety.

THE END

To follow another path, turn to page 9.
To read the conclusion, turn to page 101.

Trying to escape would be suicide. You sign. So do the other officers.

You spend the next four years in one prison camp or another. One day, you see an American pilot flying overhead. He flies low, and you see him smile. He waves and drops a chocolate bar out the window. Other planes follow. One pilot drops out his shoes and shirt for you. What wonderful gifts!

The war is over! The Allies have won, and you'll be free soon. You can't wait to see Canada again.

THE END

To follow another path, turn to page 9.
To read the conclusion, turn to page 101.

You refuse to sign. Japanese guards tie you to a tree. For two days, they give you no food or water. "Sign!" they say, and you finally agree.

You are weak. The men in your hut insist that you go to the hospital. Thank goodness the camp hospital has remained open. The doctors and nurses who shipped over with you continue to do their work, even though they are prisoners too.

At the hospital, a kind and gentle nurse takes care of you. The two of you plan to marry when you get well. But you don't get well. You develop a fever and die in the hospital one year after you arrived in Hong Kong.

THE END

To follow another path, turn to page 9.
To read the conclusion, turn to page 101.

The United States entered war
against Japan and Germany on
December 8, 1941.

CHAPTER 4

America Joins the Fight

On Sunday afternoon, December 7, 1941, you are reading a Superman comic book. The radio plays in the background. Suddenly the music stops.

"We interrupt this program to bring you a special news bulletin," a man says. "The Japanese have attacked Pearl Harbor, Hawaii, by air, President Franklin Roosevelt has just announced."

The next day, the U.S. Congress declares war on Japan. On December 9, you huddle close to the radio while President Roosevelt speaks to the nation.

Turn the page.

"We expect to eliminate the danger from Japan," he says. "But it would serve us ill if we accomplished that and found that the rest of the world was dominated by Hitler and Mussolini."

Suddenly everyone is talking about the war. At the movies, you watch newsreels about the fighting in Europe.

On November 11, 1942, Congress lowers the draft age from 21 to 18. "I'm joining the Navy as soon as I graduate from high school this spring," one of your friends says. "Why not join me?"

You were planning to begin college. Maybe this war will end before you are drafted.

➤ To sign up for the Navy as soon as you graduate, go to page **69**.

➤ To go to college, turn to page **74**.

You enlist in the Navy. "Do you want to be a medic?" an officer asks.

"Yes, sir," you answer. "I hope to be a doctor some day."

You go to Great Lakes Naval Base near Chicago for training. In basic training, you learn how to shoot a rifle and defend yourself.

Then you attend a special school to become a pharmacist's mate. This training allows you to perform first aid and nursing duties. When your training is complete, you report for duty.

"Take the train to San Diego," an officer tells you.

"Where am I going?" you ask.

"You'll know when you get there," an officer says. "In time of war, we keep information secret."

Turn the page.

In San Diego, you board an old luxury liner. The Navy is using the ship to carry soldiers to war. It is your first time on a boat, and you and everyone else are seasick. After a few days, you feel better. Many of the people on your boat are medics, nurses, or doctors. There is also a Marine division headed to battle. You enjoy beating the Marines at card games.

It takes nearly 30 days to reach the Solomon Islands in the South Pacific. You stop at Guadalcanal to drop off troops. You pick up more Marines and go to Choiseul Island. The Japanese occupy Choiseul.

On October 28, 1943, you watch as Marines land on Choiseul to attack the Japanese. The troops on your ship go ashore by boat. When they are wounded, you care for them. By the battle's end, 13 Marines and 143 Japanese soldiers are dead.

Soldiers recovered from injuries on U.S. Navy hospital ships.

A few months later, you transfer to a Navy hospital ship, the USS *Relief*. The ship, painted white with red crosses all along the side, is big enough to treat 1,000 wounded soldiers at a time. It carries 120 medical corpsmen like you, 20 doctors, and 12 Navy nurses.

Between battles, you prepare medicines, sharpen needles, and make bandages. During battles, you don't have time for anything except treating wounded soldiers.

Turn the page.

As the war continues, the ship goes wherever the Marines, Navy, or Army is fighting. The ship transports wounded soldiers and sailors to hospitals in Hawaii.

In January 1945, your ship is one of almost 900 ships headed for Iwo Jima. The island is only about 650 miles from Tokyo, Japan's largest city.

"We're taking more than 110,000 Marines to attack Japan," an officer says. "No foreign army has ever beaten the Japanese on their own territory. We'll be the first."

It takes 40 days to reach Iwo Jima. At 2:00 in the morning on February 19, Navy ships fire on Iwo Jima. An hour later, the smoke is so thick that it's hard to breathe. In the brief lull, American planes bomb the island.

U.S. troops used underwater vehicles to reach Iwo Jima's shore.

"I've counted more than 100 of our planes," another American soldier yells. "And more are coming." Once the planes fly over, the ships begin firing their big guns again.

At 8:30, your commander sends the landing force to shore. Some medics have to stay on the ship. Others will go with the landing force.

To go ashore, turn to page **81**.

To wait onboard the ship, turn to page **86**.

You graduate from high school in 1942 and take a summer job in a weapons factory. Many factories are helping with the war effort. In the fall, you begin college classes. But in November 1942, you are drafted into the U.S. Army.

You report to Fort Dix in New Jersey for two weeks of basic training. Then you go to Fort Bragg, North Carolina, where you train to be a cannoneer in a field artillery unit. You learn how to move, assemble, and fire a howitzer. It takes almost a dozen men to handle this huge gun.

Howitzers were large and powerful weapons.

On August 19, 1943, you board USS *Henry Gibbins*. You are so seasick that you can't eat. You want to sleep, but your bunk is tiny. Every time you roll over, you hit your head on the bunk above.

The trip seems to last forever. Finally on September 2, 1943, the ship pulls into port. "Where are we?" you ask.

"Oran. It's in Algeria," someone says.

"Algeria? That's in North Africa. Are we fighting here?"

"Not anymore. The British already won this battle before we could get here."

You spend several weeks waiting for orders. Meanwhile, you camp beneath the hot desert sun. Sandstorms bury your cooking gear, and you are always shaking sand out of your shoes.

Turn the page.

Finally the commanding officer calls you together. "We have our orders," he says. "We're going to Italy to fight the Germans."

Three Landing Ship Tanks (LSTs) carry you across the Mediterranean Sea to Italy. You join with the 194th Field Artillery Group of the Fifth Army.

"Bring on the war!" you yell, but what comes first is rain. Mud makes the going impossible. The big guns tip over and get stuck. You are so tired that you crawl under a canvas tarp and sleep in the mud.

You awake to German soldiers firing on you from the surrounding hills. You fire back. The gunfire is so constant and loud that your ears hurt. The air is smoky. A nearby tank blows up, hit by German missiles. Another tank blocks the road.

You fight until December 25. On Christmas Day, the Army supplies a special Christmas dinner, packages from home, and a shipment of rain boots. After one day of rest, it's back to war.

On March 23, 1943, you reach the coastal city of Anzio, Italy. The beach is full of American and British troops. The Germans are dug in on the hills above the beach. They fire 300-pound shells at you.

You dig bunkers, which are underground homes to sleep in at night. Some of the men name theirs. There's a "Holler Inn" and a "Foxhole Hotel." You call yours "Dew Drop Inn." Every morning around 4:00, German planes bomb the beach. You are always tired and ready to crawl into your bunker, out of harm's way.

Turn the page.

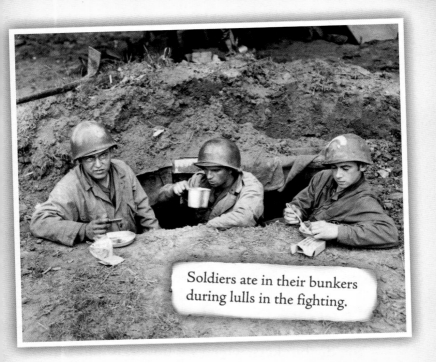

Soldiers ate in their bunkers during lulls in the fighting.

During a break one evening, a soldier from
a nearby British camp invites you to play cards.
You would enjoy a good game, but maybe you
should sleep while you can.

→ To play cards, go to page **79**.

→ To stay in camp to sleep, turn to page **92**.

78

You head off to the British camp and join your friends in a game of poker.

You play for chocolate bars. Army chocolate bars are so hard you have to break them apart with the butt of your gun. You don't mind losing chocolate.

When you return to your bunker, your friends are digging into it.

"I know he's in there," one man says.

"Who's in there?" you ask.

Everyone turns to stare at you. "You. At least we thought you were. A German shell landed directly on your bunker. We were trying to save your sorry life."

"Thanks," you say. "I may have lost the card game, but that game saved my life."

Turn the page.

British, New Zealand, and American troops fight side by side. By June 1943, the fighting at Anzio ends. You join several soldiers in a visit to Rome. Some men attend church services. Others visit the Roman ruins. The vacation is too short.

You spend another three months in Italy chasing the Germans north. In September 1943, you drive an LST to Marseilles, France. A few days later, you reach the town of Saint Benoit. You find it demolished and abandoned. Is it really abandoned? Some of the men want to check buildings for food. "It might be booby-trapped," an officer says.

➤ To stay with the main unit on the road, turn to page 89.

➤ To check the buildings, turn to page 91.

You climb over the ship's side and down a rope ladder into a small boat that takes you to shore. As soon as you hit the beach, Japanese soldiers start shooting at you from holes dug in the sand.

"Help!" a Marine shouts. He has been hit, but his wound is not serious. You call it a happy wound because he'll recover in a few days.

You bandage the soldier's wound and take him to a waiting boat. The boat will take him back to the ship for treatment. If you go along, you'll escape the worst of the fighting. But if you stay on shore, you can help other wounded men.

➤ To stay on shore, turn to page 82.

➤ To return to the hospital ship, turn to page 95.

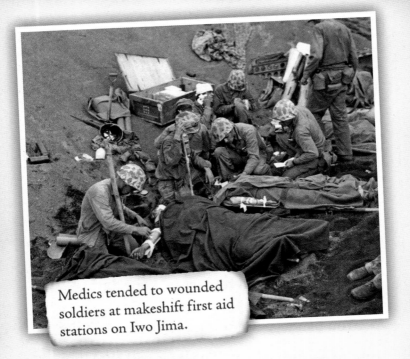

Medics tended to wounded soldiers at makeshift first aid stations on Iwo Jima.

You stay to help. Men are screaming in pain. You give first aid to several wounded soldiers.

One man dies in your arms. Others are so badly injured that they will die soon. As you rush toward another fallen soldier, you feel a searing pain in your arm. You've been shot!

"Help!" you call. A medic comes to your aid. He gives you morphine for your pain. Then he helps you back to the hospital ship.

A doctor removes the bullet. With a few days of rest, you'll recover. Most others aren't so lucky. An officer tells you, "Our company started with 310 men. Only 50 of us made it back to the ship."

When you are well enough, you go on deck and see the American flag flying over Iwo Jima.

In August 1945, a U.S. aircraft drops an atomic bomb on the Japanese city of Hiroshima. President Harry S. Truman announces the news from the cruiser USS *Augusta* in the Atlantic Ocean. He says that the bomb was more than 2,000 times more powerful than the largest bomb used to date.

A few days later, another American plane drops an atomic bomb on the Japanese city of Nagasaki. Finally the Japanese agree to surrender.

Turn the page.

The war is over! The captain orders all the ship's lights turned on. When you look over the harbor, you see thousands of Allied ships, their lights burning bright. Then every ship in the harbor fires their guns into the sky. It looks like a Fourth of July fireworks show.

Japan officially surrenders during a ceremony aboard the USS *Missouri* on September 2, 1945. Representatives from all the Allied countries are there. General Douglas MacArthur gives a speech. His chief of staff, Lieutenant General Richard Sutherland, leads the ceremony. Fleet Admiral Chester Nimitz signs on behalf of the United States.

After the war, the Allies take control of Japan to change it to a democracy. MacArthur is named supreme commander for the Allied nations.

Soldiers and sailors crowded the deck of the USS *Missouri* to watch the Japanese surrender.

Your commander asks if you would like to go with MacArthur to Japan. "You're the only one in the unit who was wounded, so the honor is yours. It's not an order. It's an invitation."

➤ *To go directly home, turn to page* **96**.

➤ *To go with MacArthur, turn to page* **98**.

Pharmacists performed tests aboard U.S. Navy hospital ships.

"I'm more useful in the lab," you say, and it's true. There are blood tests to run and medicines to prepare.

Soon boatload after boatload of wounded American soldiers reach the hospital ship. The ward is full, and you are busy giving injections to wounded soldiers.

Thanks to the skillful doctors on the ship, many seriously wounded soldiers survive the Battle of Iwo Jima. Those who don't are buried at sea with a simple ceremony.

The ship takes several trips to Hawaii to deliver wounded soldiers to hospitals. Then it returns to battle. On April 1, 1945, when the ship is in Okinawa, Japanese planes attack. You are in the middle of a delicate test when the battle alarm sounds.

➤ To go to your battle station, turn to page **88**.

➤ To finish the test, turn to page **93**.

The test will have to wait. You run to your battle station. Once it is secured, you notice a plane going by, and then another. Two Japanese pilots fly their planes into the deck of the USS *South Dakota* nearby. Flames erupt, burning several soldiers. The ship's firefighters get control of the fire. The ship survives.

After the Battle of Okinawa ends, your ship goes to the Philippines. It picks up troops going to Japan for a planned invasion. But the invasion never comes. After American planes drop atomic bombs on two Japanese cities in August, Japan surrenders. At last, the war is over.

THE END

To follow another path, turn to page 9.
To read the conclusion, turn to page 101.

You stay on the road while others run toward the village. Suddenly you hear a large boom. "The town is booby-trapped!" an officer yells.

The Germans left traps as they retreated. Bombs explode as troops accidentally set them off.

One of your friends is buried beneath the rubble. "Help!" he screams. You dig through the rock until you find him. You carefully pull him out.

"Your leg is crushed," you say. "But you'll live." That was a close call. You hope this war ends soon before you lose any of your friends.

In December 1944, you reach Germany and cross the Rhine River. You continue to fight the German Army on their home soil. They seem as tired of war as you are.

Turn the page.

On May 7, 1945, Germany surrenders. The Allies declare May 8 as Victory in Europe (V-E) Day. The Germans have surrendered. The European part of the war is over.

You spend several weeks in Oberammergau, Germany, waiting for your official release papers. While you are waiting, you learn that the Germans killed millions of Jewish people.

"They set up concentration camps where they killed their Jewish neighbors," a soldier tells you. "We went into one of the camps. The people who were still alive were starving."

You've seen enough death to last a lifetime. You want to go home. But an officer asks if you will consider fighting in the Pacific.

➤ *To wait in Germany for your release papers, turn to page **96**.*

➤ *To go to the Pacific to fight, turn to page **97**.*

You go from one bombed-out building to another hoping to find something to eat. Then you hear a chicken cluck. A fresh egg would be a treat. As you step into the barn, your leg brushes against a wire.

BOOM! The barn was booby-trapped, and you've just set it off. You die instantly.

THE END

To follow another path, turn to page 9.
To read the conclusion, turn to page 101.

You're exhausted. Constant artillery fire keeps you up all night. So you crawl into your bunker and collapse on your cot. You are sleeping soundly when the Germans start firing.

A shell lands directly on your bunker. You're buried beneath the rubble. The men of your unit dig you out, but it is too late. You were killed instantly when the shell hit. The war is over for you.

THE END

To follow another path, turn to page 9.
To read the conclusion, turn to page 101.

About 50,000 Allied soldiers were killed or wounded in the Battle of Okinawa.

You finish up the test quickly. Meanwhile, American anti-aircraft guns shoot a Japanese plane out of the sky. "We were lucky they were close by," you say to a friend.

The Battle of Okinawa is a bloody battle. For nearly three months, you work day and night treating injured soldiers.

When the battle ends in late June, more than 7,300 Americans have died. Another 32,000 are wounded. But the Japanese lost nearly 100,000 soldiers. It is a stunning defeat for the Japanese.

Turn the page.

In August, your ship heads for Japan. But on August 14, the captain makes an announcement. "We're going home. The war is over."

American planes dropped powerful atomic bombs on Japan. Thousands of Japanese people were killed. Japan's leader, Emperor Hirohito, agreed to surrender.

The ship turns around and brings soldiers back to the United States. You spend the journey treating seasick soldiers. When you reach California, you are discharged. Home at last, you're proud that you served your country.

THE END

To follow another path, turn to page 9.
To read the conclusion, turn to page 101.

There will be plenty for you to do on the ship. You help load the wounded men into the small boat for the trip back to the ship. As you are climbing into the boat, you feel a sudden pain in your chest. There's blood on your shirt.

"I've been shot!" you cry.

The wound is serious. The last sight you see is the red cross on the sleeve of a medic trying to stop the bleeding. You are one of 6,800 American soldiers who die on Iwo Jima.

THE END

To follow another path, turn to page 9.
To read the conclusion, turn to page 101.

U.S. soldiers returning from war were welcomed into New York Harbor.

It's time to go home. When your release papers arrive, you take a ship to New York. Then you catch the first train home. Mom and Dad throw a quiet celebration. You're just happy to have survived and to be with your family again.

THE END

To follow another path, turn to page 9.
To read the conclusion, turn to page 101.

You decide to sign up for service in the Pacific. In late July 1945, you reach Okinawa, an island off the coast of Japan. "We'll be invading Japan," your officer tells you.

But the invasion never comes. On August 6, 1945, the United States drops an atomic bomb on the Japanese city of Hiroshima. Three days later, the United States drops a bomb on the city of Nagasaki. Hundreds of thousands of Japanese people are injured or killed in both cities. Japanese Emperor Hirohito agrees to end the war.

On September 2, 1945, Japan officially surrenders. The war is over. You take the first available ship home and pray that there will never be another war.

THE END

To follow another path, turn to page 9.
To read the conclusion, turn to page 101.

It's an honor to join General MacArthur. You travel with MacArthur to Atsugi Air Base in Japan, between Yokohama and Tokyo.

General Douglas MacArthur commanded the occupation of Japan following the war.

One day, as you are returning to your barracks, you meet the general face-to-face. MacArthur is nearly 65 years old, but he's still strong and capable. You smile as you salute him.

After two weeks in Japan, you return by ship to San Diego. After finishing your military service, you follow your dream to become a doctor. You hope the world will never again go to war.

THE END

To follow another path, turn to page 9.
To read the conclusion, turn to page 101.

The fiery attack on Pearl Harbor on December 7, 1941, launched the United States into World War II.

CHAPTER 5

World War II

World War II took place on two fronts, in Europe and in the Pacific. It began in 1939, when Germany invaded Poland. Then Germany took over Denmark, Belgium, the Netherlands, and Norway.

In the Pacific, the Japanese attacked China in 1931 and in 1937. In 1940, Japan formed an alliance with Germany and Italy.

The United States hoped to stay out of the war. But on December 7, 1941, Japanese planes attacked Pearl Harbor, Hawaii. The next day, President Roosevelt and Congress declared war on Japan. On December 11, Germany and Italy declared war on the United States.

The United States joined the side of the Allies. The Allies included Great Britain, France, the United States, Canada, and many other countries. During the war, 1.1 million Canadians served in the armed forces. More than 16 million men and women served in the U.S. military.

The Allied invasion of Normandy in France on June 6, 1944, was a turning point in the war. From that point, the Allies regained territory in Europe, pushing the German Army back to its homeland. The war in Europe officially ended on May 8, 1945.

Meanwhile, battles raged in the Pacific. Japan won the early battles. But in June 1942, the Allies won the Battle of Midway. It was the first definite Allied victory in the Pacific. After that, the Allies pounded the Japanese military. Still, Japan refused to surrender.

Then in August 1945, the United States dropped atomic bombs on the Japanese cities of Hiroshima and Nagasaki. Between 70,000 and 100,000 people were killed in Hiroshima. About 40,000 were killed or declared missing in Nagasaki. On August 14, 1945, the Japanese agreed to surrender. They signed the surrender documents September 2, 1945. The war was over.

The United States dropped atomic bombs on two Japanese cities to end World War II.

At the end of the war, Allied troops discovered concentration camps in Germany and Poland. Between 5 and 6 million Jewish men, women, and children died in these camps. The Nazis also killed many Polish Catholics, Jehovah's Witnesses, and disabled people. After the war, German leaders were put on trial for these war crimes.

Allied troops freed sick and starving men, women, and children from German concentration camps after the war.

No one knows the exact number of people killed in World War II. Experts guess that 17 million soldiers died in battle. Even more civilians died as a result of bombing raids, massacres, and war-related illnesses. Nearly 451,000 U.S. men and women died in service.

It took years for most European countries to recover from the war. Bombed cities in Japan suffered for years after the war, as did many island nations in the Pacific.

World War II killed more people than any war in world history. It also destroyed more property and changed more lives than any other war. People everywhere continue to hope that the world will never again fight another war.

Time Line

September 1931 — Japanese troops take over the state of Manchuria in China.

July 1937 — Chinese and Japanese troops clash near Beijing, China.

September 1, 1939 — Germany invades Poland.

September 3, 1939 — Great Britain, France, Australia, and New Zealand declare war on Germany.

September 10, 1939 — Canada declares war on Germany.

April 9, 1940 — Germany invades Norway and Denmark.

May 10, 1940 — Germany invades France, the Netherlands, Belgium, and Luxembourg.

106

June 10, 1940 — Italy declares war on Great Britain and France.

June 14, 1940 — German troops enter Paris, France.

July 10, 1940 — Battle of Britain begins.

September 27, 1940 — Germany, Italy, and Japan unite as the Axis powers.

May 1941 — Germany stops bombing Great Britain, ending the Battle of Britain.

December 7, 1941 — Japan bombs Pearl Harbor, Hawaii.

December 8, 1941 — The United States, Canada, and Great Britain declare war on Japan.

December 11, 1941 — Germany and Italy declare war on the United States.

December 25, 1941 — Hong Kong surrenders to the Japanese.

September 3, 1943 — Italy surrenders to the Allies.

June 6, 1944 — Allies stage D-Day invasion of Normandy in France.

February 19, 1945 — U.S. forces land on Iwo Jima, off the coast of Japan.

April 1, 1945 — U.S. forces invade the Japanese island of Okinawa.

May 7, 1945 — Germany surrenders to the Allies.

May 8, 1945 — The war in Europe officially ends. This day becomes known as V-E (Victory in Europe) Day.

August 6, 1945 — The United States drops an atomic bomb on Hiroshima, Japan.

August 9, 1945 — The United States drops an atomic bomb on Nagasaki, Japan.

September 2, 1945 — Japan signs surrender papers. World War II is over.

OTHER PATHS TO EXPLORE

In this book, you've seen how the events experienced during World War II look different from three points of view.

Perspectives on history are as varied as the people who lived it. You can explore other paths on your own to learn more about what happened. Seeing history from many points of view is an important part of understanding it.

Here are some ideas for other World War II points of view to explore:

+ Many European Jews went into hiding to avoid the Nazis. What would it have been like to spend two or three years hiding in a small French town or on a Dutch farm?

+ Life at home in Canada or the United States was not easy during the war. Brothers, husbands, and fathers were away serving in the military. What would life have been like for families waiting at home?

+ Germany was considered the enemy of the United States. However, many Germans arrived in North America during the years before the war. What was life like for them?

READ MORE

Drez, Ronald J. *Remember D-Day: The Plan, the Invasion, Survivor Stories*. Washington, D.C.: National Geographic, 2004.

Hynson, Colin. *World War II: A Primary Source History*. Milwaukee: Gareth Stevens, 2006.

Judge, Lita. *One Thousand Tracings: Healing the Wounds of World War II*. New York: Hyperion, 2007.

Millman, Isaac. *Hidden Child*. New York: Farrar, Straus and Giroux, 2005.

INTERNET SITES

FactHound offers a safe, fun way to find educator-approved Internet sites related to this book.

Here's what you do:

1. Visit *www.facthound.com*
2. Choose your grade level.
3. Begin your search.

This book's ID number is 9781429623445.

FactHound will fetch the best sites for you!

GLOSSARY

Allies (AL-eyz) — a group of countries that fought together in World War II; some of the Allies were the United States, Canada, Great Britain, and France.

Axis powers (AK-siss POU-urz) — a group of countries including Germany, Italy, and Japan that fought together in World War II

commander (kuh-MAN-duhr) — a person who leads a group of people in the armed forces

concentration camp (kahn-suhn-TRAY-shuhn KAMP) — a camp where people such as prisoners of war, political prisoners, or refugees are held

grenade (gruh-NAYD) — a small bomb that can be thrown or launched

110

neutral (NOO-truhl) — not taking sides

partisan (PART-ih-zuhn) — a person engaged in warfare not as part of a regular army but as an independent unit

ration (RASH-uhn) — the amount of food or supplies allowed by a government

traitor (TRAY-tuhr) — someone who turns against his or her country

BIBLIOGRAPHY

Bercuson, David J. *Maple Leaf Against the Axis: Canada's Second World War.* Toronto: Stoddart, 1995.

Eman, Diet, with James Schaap. *Things We Couldn't Say.* Grand Rapids, Mich.: W. B. Eerdmans, 1994.

Klempner, Mark. *The Heart Has Reasons: Holocaust Rescuers and Their Stories of Courage.* Cleveland: Pilgrim Press, 2006.

McManus, John C. *The Deadly Brotherhood: The American Combat Soldier in World War II.* Novato, Calif.: Presidio, 1998.

Mulvey, Deb, ed. *We Pulled Together — and Won!* Greendale, Wisc.: Reiman, 1993.

Wheeler, William J., ed. *Flying Under Fire.* Calgary, Alberta: Fifth House, 2001.

INDEX